C000084869

Perception Is Reality

Stefon Williams

ISBN: 9798504180434

What They See Is What They'll Be

10% of the proceeds from this book will be donated to The 100 Black Men of London, a community-based charity, led by Black men, that empowers young Black people to be the best versions of themselves.

Since their inception in 2001, The 100 have been uplifting the Black community through their four pillars for the future: Mentoring, Economic Empowerment, Health and Wellbeing, and Education.

Their services are delivered by their dedicated members and volunteers (men and women) who go above and beyond for their community.

You can find out more about The 100, and the wonderful work they do, via their website: 100bmol.org.uk.

Together We Can.

Thank You

I truly believe almost anything, including writing a book, is possible with a strong support network.

I am sincerely thankful to:

Nana Dickson,
For walking with me on my writing journey, from the days I was writing positive mantras on Instagram under the name @Positive_Stef (let's laugh together); for opening your mind to my work (we both know poetry in its purest form isn't cool where we're from); for being a supportive reader, a great friend, a loving brother.

Karuna Gujadhur,
For your endless encouragement and belief in my talent; you were convinced I could write a book that could impact and inspire many and thanks to you I'm now convinced, too.

Everyone who has supported me,
I know I sometimes (majority of the time) act like I don't need any support but trust me, I do; without yours, it's very likely this book wouldn't have happened.

The world changes according to the way people see it, and if you alter, even by a millimetre, the way a person looks at reality, then you can change it.

James Baldwin

Contents

Part 4

Part 1

Reconnecting

I've had a love for words since primary school. It was there I learned how powerful they are, especially when it came to cussing fellow pupils who got on my nerves. My choice of words had got me into a few altercations which forced me to reconsider my language, so from a young age I've appreciated why it's important for everyone, especially skinny people who can't fight, to choose their words wisely.

It was at primary school I first read *The Suitcase Kid* by Jacqueline Wilson, a brilliant story which opened my imagination. I was in awe of how Wilson had created a movie in my mind with just words – simple words, words I could understand, words I could write. Thus, the seeds for my own storytelling were sowed and whenever my class was given free-time, I spent mine writing stories.

I would love to tell you that from then until now I've been on a storytelling journey, writing book after book, but, unfortunately, I haven't. I consigned my childhood love for creative writing to the "childish" phase of my life, and from secondary school onwards I directed my energy to more serious forms of writing – writing essays (which was cool but not as fun as writing stories) and then monotonous work emails and reports. Choosing words became a chore rather than a pleasure.

I was in my mid-twenties when I seriously asked myself "why have I fallen out of love with my life?"; note that I didn't ask myself the proverbial, "what am I doing with my life?" - I had been asking myself that since I was a teenager in college and was none the wiser in my twenties. It didn't take me long to realise that my life felt unfulfilled because I wasn't doing anything I really enjoyed, but it did take me a while to work out what that thing I really enjoy doing is.

I came across a book, the name I can't remember, which advised those who are trying to find their joy to trace their mind back to their childhood, when they were free from responsibility, and to recall what it was they enjoyed doing then. Bingo! I enjoyed playing kiss-chase haha. Ok seriously, my mind landed on creative writing, of course (although, I must admit, I would be a lot more successful playing kiss chase now than I was back then).

When I was going through my mid-twenties crisis, my mind was filled with self-help style wisdom which I had been saying to myself for motivation. Whilst scrolling through Instagram and taking in the usual scenery, mainly half-naked women, I occasionally saw motivational quotes that were attracting tonnes of likes. This is interesting, I thought, and a potential path for me to follow. So, I decided to set up my own Instagram motivational account, @Positive_Stef (don't bother searching for it; I deleted it). I used it to share my own quotes and when I started getting positive feedback, I realised I had a gift for impacting others with my writing, even though my following was small.

My dear friend, Sarah, spotted this first and she implored me to create a blog; after much hesitation, I followed her advice. Thus, www.snwrites.blog was born. I used this blog to share my poetry and reflections, and I would later use it to occasionally share film reviews. With the help of some great friends – especially Fola and Nana, who regularly gave me feedback on my work and shared it on their networks – I was able to reach more people with my writing (on some days I would get over a hundred visits on my blog).

My writing appeared to be going in a positive direction, but, as I often do, I doubted myself. I told myself that my writing wasn't that good, and, even if it was, it wouldn't go that far and it would never make me money. I had still associated creative writing with the "childish" part of my life and I felt, as an adult, I should be doing more serious things, like researching index tracker funds, and stocks and shares. So, I ended up wiping all my material off my website and slipping back into an empty, adult, existence centred on work.

Since then, I've been going through what many would describe as an "awakening", or a "healing" process. The things I had forced to the back of my mind have come forward and forced me to face them. I've been coming to terms with the trauma of losing my dad when I was just two-years-old; the agony of seeing my mum suffer severely from sickle cell; dealing with homelessness; and, in 2017, a childhood friend was murdered. With no outlet, this pain has pent up inside me. So now, like an ex-drug addict desperate to be high again, I've returned to writing for relief.

This time, I'm clear on what I'm doing and why, and I'm a lot more confident. I must write for myself, and for those who can relate to my experience, and for those who can't. I must write everyday, if possible. I must write even when I don't have a device or a pen in my hand; I must write with my mind and my heart, because they're all I really need to write.

I previously struggled with publicity - I couldn't think of anything worse than "being out there", especially for prolonged periods - but I'm realising that true joy is found outside comfort zones. In perhaps the biggest step I've ever taken out of mine, I've written and published this book, partly because I want to share my writing, *my gift*, with the world before my time on it is up, so that it can, I hope, bless everyone who reads it and live forever in their hearts and minds.

And above all, I want to enjoy life again.

A Greater Good

We were chilling on the low wall behind Gran's block, taking a break from one of my cousin's adventures. *We,* on this summer afternoon, was a primary school me (I can't remember how old I was), my cousin, who is older than me by a few years, and his friend, a white boy, from a nearby block.

It came out of nowhere like a ball that fell from the sky.

"Where is your dad", my cousin's friend casually asked, looking at me. There was no malice in his eyes, just curiosity. Caught off guard, I let the question bounce in silence for a moment as my mum's voice echoed in my mind - *don't tell anyone our business*. My cousin, sensing an opportunity, eagerly caught the question and ran with it.

"His dad got killed fighting in a war", he said with a smile as big as the lie he just told. I watched his and his friend's eyes fill with excitement as he spoke about how good my dad was with guns and how he was a top-ranked solider. *This is why my mum tells me to stay away from you*, I thought. What came out of his uncontrollable mouth next, I can't remember; the most important detail of this memory is war.

Significant parts of my childhood felt like a war comprised of many battles. *Don't speak to them, they don't like us*, my mum would often warn me about family; *last one out is a loser*, the kids on the block would say as we played FA (knockouts) on the concrete battlefield; *Welcome to Monday Night Raw is War*, Jim Ross would scream from the TV screen every Friday night. Like a solider, I had no choice but to embrace the battles. It would be extreme to say my survival depended on how I came through them but they were certainly instrumental to my growth.

One battle I never got accustomed to was the absence of my dad; my mum tried as hard as she could to fight this battle for us both. I wonder if it would have been easier if he had been a typical absent-father, aware of who and where I was but fighting his own battles, because no matter how difficult a battle is, there's always a chance you can come through it if you're alive. But my dad wasn't alive; he had lost his life in what I now consider a war.

Wars involve people killing each other. My dad was, I've been told, shot dead by another man in Jamaica. My gran tells me he was a kind man which meant, for a long time, his death didn't make sense to me because why would anyone want to kill a kind man? I eventually learned that war seldom makes sense. I know my dad was killed for a reason, one I don't understand, and never will, but the image of him dying in a war fighting for a cause, for a greater good, gives me solace, however fanciful it may be, and it helps me make sense of the senseless.

Rest in Peace
Dad.

My birth certificate says you was a painter.
I paint pictures with words.

Love Thy Neighbourhood

Wednesday, November 16, 2011

I rarely take an interest in the tabloids but today one caught my attention. I was walking down the high street, heading for the train that takes me to university, when I saw a copy of The Daily Mirror on the floor, pages flapping in the wind. On the front page I saw my reflection under the headline:

**SWALLOWED
BY TIDE
OF HATE**
MURDER TRIAL TOLD HOW GANG SAVAGED STEPHEN LAWRENCE

I picked up the newspaper and, being someone who appreciates creative writing, I reflected on the choice of words. *Tide of hate.* I would have gone for *tsunami of hate,* instead; tsunamis are more destructive.

Stephen was half-smiling at me, at the world, from that now iconic pic in which he's wearing a navy blue and white striped t-shirt. I couldn't bring myself to smile back; I never can when I see his face. But I can say that he did have good taste. I have a short-sleeved shirt with the same pattern; it's one of my favourites.

Next to his face was a picture of his mum's but she wasn't smiling; Doreen Lawrence wore a serious and disappointed expression, one my mum also wears – my gran says she's worn it ever since my dad was killed.

Below the picture of Doreen Lawrence, the headline story started:

**MURDERED Stephen Lawrence
was "swallowed up" by a racist
knife gang who stabbed him to
death, a court heart yesterday.**

The "racist knife gang" *swallowed* him up yet it's me and many others who feel personally affected by Stephen's death who are left struggling to digest it; it's stuck in my throat like a lump of food too big to pass through my body.

I couldn't read the rest of the story because it was making me sick and I knew how it would end – without justice, so I scrunched the paper into a ball and threw it in a nearby bin which had a sign on it that said: *Love Your Neighbourhood*. I reflected on this commandment. Why Should we love a neighbourhood, a society, that doesn't love us in return? We don't have any more cheeks to turn.

Who Are We?

Our suffering has become so normal and
consistent that we seek it when it's missing.

If it's gone for too long we bring it upon
ourselves so that we can feel in control of it,
for once.

It's the conflict in our life stories; what
story worth telling doesn't have conflict?

It's our truth. Let them not lie and say it isn't;
they haven't experienced it like us, if at all.

It's interwoven into our identities so we
must wear it with a pained pride, unless
we decide to hide who we are,
where we're from,
what we've been through,
behind a carefully constructed costume.

Who are we without our suffering?

True Colours

In a Black and White world
in which there are *two types of people*
I wonder how I can show my true colours.

I used to escape the Black and White world
by drinking from the deep blue sea of hope
(I once saw a colourful future at the bottom)
but I had to stop because drinking sea water
is toxic for the human body, apparently.

I tried changing the Black and White world
but my paint brush wore thin and
now I'm left with just my red heart
which burns every day with a desire to set the
Black and White world on fire
so that we can all start again.

Part 2

Sandcastle

He dreamed of going to the beach on a sunny day
to play and build a sandcastle
as big as the one he lived on.
When he asked his mum if they can go
she said, *No, that's for white people;*
we don't need British sun and sand,
we have plenty back home.

Feeling sorry, she decided he was
now old enough to go outside and
play on the yellow brick estate,
a desert where children are exposed to,
and unprotected from,
the street's unforgiving heat.

Escapism

Feeling trapped on the estate, he was determined to escape. He knew what he wanted to leave behind – the rats that lived rent-free in the tiny two-bedroom council flat he shared with his mum; the pissy stairwells he had to use when the lifts were down (which was always); being chased by gangs who thought he was an opp. He wanted to put all these things and more in his rear-view but he didn't have a destination in mind; where exactly he was going he didn't know - he just wanted to go as far away as possible from the endz and not be poor anymore.

He was watching Paid In Full as he laid on his single bed with his feet hanging over the edge when he devised a plan; "I'm gonna pick up some grams and hustle my way out", he declared to himself.

The following night, he stood on the street corner for the first time like a novice with white powder in his pockets, dreaming of the vast profit he would make from his neighbourhood's addiction, but his dreams hadn't revealed to him the friction that comes with the late nights and long days, the frantic fiends, the conniving competition, the dogged DIs.

When the money started coming in his life started changing, but not in the way he expected. He was now more respected on the endz and he felt financially free (as free as a boy can be with his money hidden at different locations across London) but he didn't feel like he was making real progress; he hadn't left the endz.

He had skilfully/luckily avoided police traps and jumped over hurdles, but he felt he had gone full circle back to the estate he tried so hard to escape. He begun doubting if he would ever leave it, and if it would ever leave him.

The Corner & The Predictable Ending

With his back to the wall
he stood on the edge of the corner
made ends meet on the corner
helped Mum pay her bills from the corner
fed his kids from the corner
but never let them play on the corner.

In the corner of his mind he knew that
a life on the corner is short-lived but
he carried on, convinced, a better life
was just around the corner.

In perhaps the most predictable ending
to a story you'll ever read

                              he met his end on the corner.

Now they cry on the corner
leave flowers on the corner
write RIP on the corner.

15

Dead To The World

Filled with frustration, they pour themselves into an empty
existence which affirms their invisible status.

They are ghosts of their future, better, selves,
dead to what they could have been,
what they could have been dead to the world.

Shattered Mirror

In the shattered mirror I see
my broken reflections,
distorted, silently screaming for my help;
in their eyes I recognise
an ignorant pride and an ignored pain.

I tried to pull them all out but
they tried to pull me in, so I had no choice
but to pull away and save myself.

Now I feel a survivor's guilt
when I look from afar in the shattered mirror.

Salvation

Four of our teenage boys have been killed this month by their brothers who are being controlled by the Devil. We cannot let him win; we cannot let him continue to divide us and wreak havoc in our community. We must come together and ask the Lord for salvation.

The Devil has had a good month.

Four lives have ended before they've started; four more Black boys have joined the Dearly Departed. Four mums and/or dads will bury their sons in the ground and themselves in guilt and they'll ask, what could I have done to prevent my son from being killed? The pastor's answer will be, "we must give ourselves to God and encourage our boys to seek salvation, because through salvation we have eternal life with God in heaven after death".

The pastor's words seem profound - they've got people on their feet, some are in tears – but I can't hear them as he wants me to. His words float around me like a spirit struggling to find a way in but I have no space for them at the moment, no space for an eternal after-life in heaven when life right now, right here on earth, feels like it's trapped in hell.

The tragic deaths of these four boys means so many things, and as the pastor speaks about the Devil and prayer and salvation, I start to wonder if I've been *saved* - how else could I have survived after committing *suicide* four times this month?

Autumn All Year

In a garden as big as London there is a beautiful tree which stands tall but, unfortunately, it's stuck in autumn all year; every day it sheds leaves but it does so *unnaturally*.

Each time a Black boy causes another Black boy to bleed in the garden, a leaf on the tree turns red, and if this loss of blood results in a loss of life, the red leaf falls to the ground and is pulled through the concrete, deep into the soil.

We won't know why this happens unless we get close to the tree and study its root. We must understand where it comes from and acknowledge (not hide from) the fact that something unnatural has happened in its growth.

Telling yourself this tree has the potential to grow to the same height as other trees is true, in theory, but in reality this tree will forever remain in the shadows of others unless we nourish its roots with love and tend to its weak branches with compassion.

Life After Death

In the white, merciless, eyes of the system,
a Black boy's life begins the moment
he allegedly commits his first crime;
this is the point at which his existence
is first recognised.

Although the boy entered the world years before this point,
his life before then is treated as if it existed in another world.

The law, which is supposedly concerned with justice,
looks only at the crime the boy is accused of committing
and not at the crimes society has committed against him,
meaning the boy, who is a victim as much as, if not more than,
he is a perpetrator, begins a life after death,
a death of conscience and empathy.

Letter To My Brothers

Dear Brothers,

I write as I see your familiar faces on the news again and I can no longer pretend that our worlds are apart.

I know how it feels to be misrepresented and resented for just being a boy who is Black, and to see those who can relate turn their back, yet I turned mine on you. I admit, I had time for myself and others but never time for you.

I have no explanation other than both pride and shame can separate people who are much the same.

Please forgive me for acting like I forgot what it's like to be forgotten. I was caught between the top and the bottom but that's no excuse; I must now face the truth - you are a reflection of myself lacking direction and my help.

I pushed for diversity in the workplace but did nothing when I saw you dying on the streets in the worst way, and it hurts me to say I failed you. So now I apologise and avail you of my time and love, because there's no justice, it's just us.

Yours sincerely,

Your Brother

Gamechangers

Tired of blaming our environment and poverty we wanted to break free, but, unlike our olders, we wanted to do it properly. We had dreams of owning businesses and property and, most importantly, our time. Our olders owned nice cars but they couldn't really go anywhere because they were stuck on their grind. They thought they were free but really they were slaves to the streets, forever hustling so they could buy symbols of freedom to wear around their necks and on their feet.

We had a plan to do it different, so we kept our distance from the olders. Now free from their backward ways of thinking we merged our minds and a new vision emerged. We wanted to fly but not by riding birds; we wanted to be high but not on a drug supply.

We wanted to be the guys to change the narrative, so that no matter how bad it gets for our youngers, they can see us and be inspired to dream bigger and do better.

We wanted to change the game.

Community Callout

A few years ago, in one of those summers where it seems the media have nothing to report on except a surge in knife crime across London, I came across a flyer from The Nation of Islam on Instagram - it was an invitation to discuss solutions to the youth violence problem in "*our* community". It held my attention for two reasons: one, I had heard so much about the Nation of Islam but knew little about them; two, they were focused on finding solutions to a problem I felt affected by.

Without thinking much about whether the event was meant for me, I decided to attend. I lived a few miles from Brixton, the location for the event; I had lived experience of youth violence; and I always had a good relationship with Muslims, perhaps because I looked Somali - I've lost count of the number of times Somalians have greeted me in Arabic and I've awkwardly replied "Hi".

When I arrived at the venue that night, I was sure I had read either the address or the date for the event wrong. I stood alone outside what appeared to be a door painted on a wall on a backstreet in Loughborough, Brixton - not a place you want to be hanging around for too long with no good reason. After a few knocks from me, the door opened and I was welcomed in by two, young, Black men, smartly dressed in black suits, ties and shiny shoes. In my check shirt and Nike Air Max trainers, I felt out of place but they quickly made me feel comfortable.

On the way up a flight of narrow stairs, they engaged me in conversation that normally feels insignificant, "how are you?", "how was your journey?", but here it felt more meaningful, like a conversation between brothers who hadn't seen each other in a while. I smiled when I reached the top and saw more Black men, young and old, all smartly dressed; they all smiled back. Was this the Nation of Islam deemed a threat to society?

As always, I was early. About thirty minutes after my arrival the hundred or so empty seats in the main hall began to fill. It didn't take long for there to not be enough seats for everyone. At the request of The Nation, men stood up and offered their seats to women and children; I must admit, this courtesy wouldn't have crossed my mind without their prompt.

When everyone was settled, I looked at the audience with a mix of pain and pride. It hurt to see that almost everyone in attendance was Black. I knew for a long time that street violence in South London (and other parts of London) predominantly affected young Black people (particularly boys), but it hurt nonetheless to see the scale of the problem in one room. And at the same time, it made me proud to see so many Black people come together with a common desire to find solutions.

As the night proceeded, men and women, young and old, shared their thoughts and feelings and particularly their pain at seeing our young people kill each other. Some parents tearfully told the audience that their lives hadn't been the same since their sons were killed. At times, it was a lot to take in, but I was there to hear it raw from those who were most affected and to hear from them, from everyone, suggestions for solutions. What struck me most was the language that was commonly used. The words *we* and *our* were used a lot but not meaninglessly. W*e must do something and save our children*; I felt like I was at a family crisis meeting and I was a key part of the family.

What I don't recall hearing is the divisive phrase "black-on-black crime". There seemed to be no need for it. Everyone present seemed aware that the violence happening in our community was being inflicted by black boys on each other, by our sons, our brothers, our nephews, our cousins. No one was concerned with academic debates about inner-city youth violence, citing examples from Glasgow and Scotland, and much to my surprise there was hardly any talk about systemic racism. We were primarily concerned with what *our* community could do in the present moment to stop the violence. There was no looking outwards for solutions (to state intervention, for example), not that solutions outside the community didn't exist; they did, and still do, in my opinion anyway, but to discuss them wasn't why the community had been brought together. It wasn't to ask what the government could do; it was to ask what the people most affected could do. Since that night, this call for community action, for collective responsibility, has echoed in my mind, causing me to constantly consider how can we, can I, help our young people avoid a life of violence?

Breaking Barriers

If our goal is to develop our whole community, how much impact can we really make if we only engage with people who we perceive to be on our level? How much progress can we make if our rich people only talk with each other, and our spiritual people do the same? If our aim is to collectively break through barriers, we must first break the ones between us and those who need us the most in our community.

Until we are all free, none of us are free – Emma Lazarus (I heard Jay-Z say it first)

Aligned

Please, can we stop waiting
for the stars to align
and for a perfect time
that doesn't exist.
Instead, let's believe
that we have everything we need
right here and now
to somehow open the doors
we hoped would open for us.

Remembering Grenfell

We cried and filled buckets
with our tears and threw them
on the flames that were
fanned by their neglect
but our tears did nothing

except water the soil
out of which we grew again.

Part 3

Cracks

When I hear you struggling with the voices in your head, I wish they would talk to me instead so you can have peace.

Maybe they prefer the challenge of breaking you down because you've appeared strong for so long, but I know beneath the surface you're fragile. I've known this for a while, yet I've been hard on you, which, I now regretfully realise, has made you crack more.

But you don't have to hide your cracks anymore, not from me, because I know that even the tallest buildings, the ones which have withstood the heaviest winds, have cracks on them somewhere. I know this because I'm one of them.

A Message From The Past

My dear friend
why do you look so troubled?
I understand you for I once stood
at the crossroads you now stand.
For you, I made a self-sacrifice;
I endured life so you can enjoy life.

Like me, you're a warrior
capable of overcoming life's toughest battles.
Please don't stress over the future
and where you'll be;
I once stressed over you and
now you're in a better place than me.

At Peace With The Past

To find peace, I had to forgive myself for not being where I thought I should be in life. This shifted my focus from looking back and trying to close the gap, to accepting where I am and understanding why. I now understand that I'm exactly where I'm meant to be, whether I like it or not. At peace with my past, I now look forward, living each moment fully in the present, with hope and no regret.

A Better View

Think
of how high you could be
and how much you could see, if you
stood on top of everything that's holding you down.

Perception Is Reality

We can't change what happened
but with perception
we can change *why* it happened.

Through perception we can give new meaning
to the past and change the course of the future.

Perception has the power to turn:

*losses into
lessons*

*obstacles into
opportunities*

*setbacks into
success.*

Perception is reality.

Passion

When I was in a dark place, a met a beautiful woman called Passion. At the time I met her I was seeing Distraction, who was holding me back and blocking me from my destiny, but Passion is different, she only wants what's best for me.

Passion is truly one of a kind; she has set my soul on fire and opened my mind. She has pulled me through pain and adversity and shown me how much Distraction was hurting me.

I wondered how my life would've been if I'd met Passion when I was in my teens, but I stopped looking back on what I never had when I found so much to look forward to.

Evolution

As I evolved
my dreams became goals
my thinking became planning
my words became actions
my focus overcame distractions.

Part 4

Heavy

Growing up as a Black boy in South London was a heavy experience. For the 90s babies who remember heavy being a positive term, another slang for cool, I'm using the word with its literal meaning - *of great weight, difficult to lift or move*; although, I must say, it was cool being a Black boy, sometimes - sometimes being the times we weren't mistreated for what appeared to be no other reason than the fact we were Black boys.

I became conscious of this weight in secondary school, often a make-or-break period in the formative years for teenagers, especially Black, male, teenagers. My school was an advert of inner-city multiculturalism; the type that doesn't necessarily come with inclusion. The Latin boys had their own corner in the playground and us Black boys ran the whole playground, literally. You could find us playing football with a tennis ball in large groups (sometimes up to fifty of us), or at the one basketball hoop on the school grounds, being American Black boys. In the summertime, during Wimbledon season, you could find us playing *4 Square* – a strategic game that tested our brotherhood. I wouldn't describe these moments of joy as heavy, though; I'd say they were the rare times we felt free at school.

It was the loneliness I felt despite there being so many of us that felt heavy. This loneliness, which I haven't spoken of until now, was felt in two ways. It was felt collectively, by a group that made up a large portion of the school population but felt like a minority. What does being in a minority feel like? It feels like having decisions which affect you being made by people who detest you. This is a strong accusation, I know, but how else can I perceive the actions of teachers who plotted to have some of us excluded from school instead of helping us get through it? I must admit, I didn't get such a rough ride from teachers, perhaps because I was barely in school, which meant I experienced my friends' struggles vicariously through their stories on MSN messenger and Yahoo Messenger.

In the interest of fairness, I must admit that we did have some good teachers who seemed to genuinely care, but they felt like the exceptions who went against the norm. Sadly, there were few Black teachers within that exception. We never understood why they had no mercy on us; we had enough tough love at home.

The other side of this heavy loneliness was felt individually; well, it was for me. Although I had so many boys around me who looked like me, spoke like me, had similar interests, backgrounds, and upbringings as me, I felt different, and feeling different at that age, in that environment, felt like being alone in a crowd.

Struggling every day to conform to the South London standard of a teenage Black boy was mentally and physically tiring. My feet ached from chasing other Black boys, and running from them, in a street life I really wasn't built for. My face ached from screwing and my cheeks were sore from laughing at jokes which I knew deep down, despite the ignorance of youth, weren't appropriate; still I laughed, at myself more than anything, because I eagerly played the role of a clown.

GCSE results day was real heavy; perhaps my heaviest day at school, which says something because there were countless challenging days - getting home safely after school was like completing a level on Super Mario Smash Bros. When I got my envelope, which, I had been led to believe, contained my future, I opened it – away from the other students, just in case embarrassment awaited me – and looked at my grades with indifference. I finished five years of education with nine

GCSEs, which wasn't bad but nor was it great - four of them were below C and five were above. The only one I cared about was my A in English Literature. I hadn't considered my career yet but I had a feeling it would involve writing.

After school came college, which was, without a doubt, the hardest phase of my adolescence. Now given the freedom to study what I want and wear what I want, I felt like the weight on me had been lifted but I quickly learned that it hadn't; it had shifted to my A-Level textbooks. Academically, college was far more challenging and culturally it felt like a huge jump from the relative softness of secondary school. Secondary School was far from soft, but some of the teachers at least attempted to act like they cared, especially during OFSTED inspections. At college, the tutors (not teachers, we were told) told us openly that they weren't there to baby us and they meant it. They didn't bug me for homework or call home when I didn't attend lessons. College was a test of maturity, a test I failed miserably.

At the end of my first year, my grades, unsurprisingly (but I acted surprised to my mum), weren't good enough for me to advance to second year, and I was a late off the mark with reapplying for first year; the many other students who shared the misfortune of getting D grades and below beat me to it. I was officially a failure, consoled on my last day by the bulging side pockets on my combat trousers that were filled with coins from my poker and pound-up winnings (towards the end of the year, I attended college just to gamble).

Determined to fix up, I enrolled at another college, one much closer to home - too close, it would turn out. Academically I was doing well there and suddenly I had become attractive to girls. Perhaps they could sense my seriousness, my growing maturity, or perhaps they were immature for thinking I wanted anything serious with them– or maybe it was the mohawk haircut I had for a few months. At the end of this year, my grades were decent and I was ready to take on my second and final year but some *issues* from the streets spilled over into my college life, and after taking a beating from some boys, I had no choice but to leave unless I wanted to be constantly watching my back between lessons. That was a burden I wasn't willing to bear, not after seeing what I could do if I focused on my work.

On to first year number three. This time, I enrolled at a sixth form (at the non-negotiable request of my mum) at the age of eighteen, the year most students start university. The feeling of shame and embarrassment was pride-breaking heavy, as heavy as the caravans I saw the ant-like year 7s carrying on their backs as they walked through the same gate as me, asking me for directions. On my first day, my fellow sixth formers looked at me with curiosity, wondering if I was a supply teacher. To make things worse, I had to dress smart again like I was in school, in shirt, tie and trousers. When I got home at the end of each day, I would change my attire quicker than Clarke Kent when his Superman duties called. Thankfully, I got through this humbling phase of my education with three A-levels that were good enough to secure me a place at uni.

If you're expecting me to tell you of drama at uni, there was none. I breezed through it and finished with a solid degree but the feeling of being behind weighed heavy on me. The reality of finally finishing education had dawned on me long before my final exam, and when I put the pen down and left the exam hall after sitting my last paper, I went straight home and then opened my laptop and started looking for jobs. The weight of catching up, of fulfilling my potential, of just finding a job and earning money, had become unbearable.

After finishing uni, I hop-scotched through a few dull jobs and at each one I felt empty; I knew that I was doing a job I didn't enjoy but I had told myself joy wasn't important - money was. Now, I find more joy in my work but I still feel heavy. At the back of my mind, I can still feel the weight of my past mistakes, and the pressure to make up for them (self-imposed pressure, I admit). I also feel an obligation to support others, especially young people, who have been through what I have, and to help them thrive despite the pressure they're under. I feel like I'm not doing enough but at the same time I feel like I'm doing a lot. I know I will never be completely free of these pressures because they're a part of me, but I can live with them now because I recognise this. Through experience, I've learned how to not let them crush me.

Seeing The Light

From my bedroom window, I could see the lights from the Canary Wharf skyscrapers shining in the night sky like stars. Although it wasn't far, Canary Wharf felt like it was on a different planet for some reason. Perhaps it was because I had never been there, despite living relatively close, or it was the stories I had heard about the large sums of money people allegedly made there, sums that felt alien to me. Despite this distance, I told my teenage-self, half-heartedly, that I would one day work on The Wharf, for superficial reasons, of course.

Half a heart is all you need sometimes - in my mid-twenties I made it happen. After sleepwalking through a series of uninspiring post-uni jobs, I secured my place on The Wharf at an international energy company. Although I was on a modest salary, I told myself I had made it, and my friends and family agreed. It's funny how some people are quick to assume everyone who works on Canary Wharf, or in the city, earns six figures and it's funnier when you're the guy they think is now a millionaire but you're not; you just act like one, spending £7 on salt-beef sandwiches allegedly made with the finest bread for lunch, and riding boats on your commute from work.

It didn't take long for the gloss on this seemingly pristine lifestyle to wear and reveal the rusty, out-dated, machine I was just a tiny part of. Frustration found me in the form of work emails celebrating the construction of renewable energy sites – don't get me wrong, this was good news – but where was the commitment to renewing the whitewash workforce? Where was the energy of diverse talent? The Wharf was no longer exceptional; I was the exception. It wasn't out of this world, as I once thought; it was a reflection of it. This myth-busting revelation came with benefits, though. It showed me that work is something I should do, with pride and joy; it shouldn't be somewhere I go.

Tired of being pretentious, I decided to stop pretending I was living my dream and snapped out of my corporate zombie unconsciousness. It was time to be alive and not just make a living; it was time to pursue that mythical thing called *my purpose,* but I had no idea what it looked like and where to find it.

Missed Calling

I sit in my office
that isn't really mine
staring blankly at the glass ceiling
feeling
like a hostage
kept against my will.

I am numb
from the endless emails and calls
which aren't connected
to my calling
and as each day goes by
I feel like I am falling
further
into
emptiness.

Post Code Pride: An Everyday Performance

Characters: Xavier, Managing Director at Better Living Ltd, a healthcare provider; Femibola (called Femi for, ease), a new Marketing Intern at Better Living Ltd

Setting: The kitchen of Better Living Ltd's Headquarters in Central London.

Femi takes his egusi soup out the microwave as Xavier walks in.

Xavier: [Sniffing] What's that smell?

Femi:

Xavier: Hey, nice to meet you [shakes Femi's hand]. I'm Xavi; the Managing Director here. [Looks at Femi's lanyard around his neck] Ah yes, our new marketing intern. Welcome!

Femi: Thanks, It's an honour to -

Xavier: [Opening the fridge] How was your journey? Did you travel far?

Femi: No-no; one bus from Lewisham.

Xavier: [Opens smoothie bottle and sniffs the contents] Oh, Lewisham. I had a friend in who uni lived there, Kemisha; I always admired her strength. You know, it ain't easy [drinks smoothie until it's finished]. Apricot and mango, my favourite.

Femi:

Xavier: You know, all that fighting over post codes nonsense; not getting dragged in that is an achievement if you ask me. Well done. [Throws smoothie bottle in the waste bin, not the recycling bin]

Femi: I wouldn't -

Xavier: [Takes ringing phone out pocket] Ah sorry Fumbi, I've got to take this call from the estate agent. The wife and I are desperately trying to secure a four-bedroom in Richmond; we're so done with Peckham. I'll see you around [Answers phone and walks out the kitchen]

Femi:

Curtain.

Seeing The Light Continued

It was late in the night when I looked out my bedroom window and searched for the light that would lead me to my next career move; I also listened attentively for the voice that would tell me my vocation.

On the horizon, I saw the bedroom lights on the nearby high-rise estate dotted like cheese in the holes of a rusty cheese grater. I wondered what the residents on the estate, those who were awake, were thinking about. Were they searching for the same light as me?

As I got lost in my thoughts, their bedroom lights got closer, growing bigger and brighter, and then they merged into one. This light, being all I could now see, felt intentional, like it was trying to bring my attention to something I couldn't see, or didn't want to see. This light wouldn't let me be blind to *it* anymore; I could no longer be blind to *them*.

In the centre of the light an image of a high-rise emerged; it was like the orange one my gran lived on, the one I grew up on in East Street. I saw myself standing on one end of the top floor and the residents standing on the other, before we slowly started walking towards each other. We were within touching distance when the supernatural light through which I saw this image gave way to the morning sun. But the image remains. I can still see it, flickering in my cave like a burning candle that can't be put out.

Printed in Great Britain
by Amazon

64821917R00036